CAKES &
BISCUITS

RECIPE
COLLECTION
BOOK

Look out for others in this set

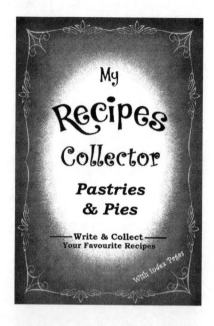

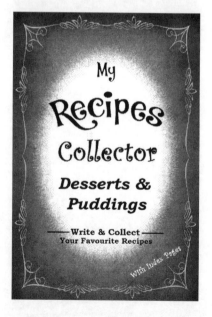

By Dunstamac & Purple Polly

TABLE OF CONTENTS

N°	RECIPE	PAGE
....	....	....
....	....	....
....	....	....
....	....	....
....	....	....
....	....	....
....	....	....
....	....	....
....	....	....
....	....	....
....	....	....
....	....	....
....	....	....
....	....	....
....	....	....
....	....	....
....	....	....
....	....	....
....	....	....
....	....	....

TABLE OF CONTENTS

TABLE OF CONTENTS

TABLE OF CONTENTS

N°	RECIPE	PAGE
....	....	....
....	....	....
....	....	....
....	....	....
....	....	....
....	....	....
....	....	....
....	....	....
....	....	....
....	....	....
....	....	....
....	....	....
....	....	....
....	....	....
....	....	....
....	....	....
....	....	....
....	....	....
....	....	....
....	....	....

Recipe:

Preparation Time: _____   Serves: _____

Oven Temp: _____ Cooking Time: _____

Ingredients

_____ _____
_____ _____
_____ _____
_____ _____
_____ _____
_____ _____
_____ _____

Method

Notes

Recipe: _____

Preparation Time: _____ Serves: _____

Oven Temp: _____ Cooking Time: _____

Ingredients

_____   _____
_____   _____
_____   _____
_____   _____
_____   _____
_____   _____
_____   _____
_____

Method

_____
_____
_____
_____
_____
_____
_____
_____

Notes

_____
_____
_____
_____
_____

Recipe: _____

Preparation Time: _____   Serves: _____

Oven Temp: _____ Cooking Time: _____

Ingredients

_____ _____
_____ _____
_____ _____
_____ _____
_____ _____
_____ _____
_____ _____

Method

_____
_____
_____
_____
_____
_____
_____
_____

Notes

_____
_____
_____
_____

Recipe:

Preparation Time: _____ Serves: _____

Oven Temp: _____ Cooking Time: _____

Ingredients

_____   _____
_____   _____
_____   _____
_____   _____
_____   _____
_____   _____
_____   _____

Method

Notes

Recipe:

Preparation Time:_____ Serves:_____

Oven Temp:_____ Cooking Time:_____

Ingredients

_____   _____
_____   _____
_____   _____
_____   _____
_____   _____
_____   _____
_____   _____
_____   _____

Method

_____
_____
_____
_____
_____
_____
_____
_____
_____

Notes

_____
_____
_____
_____
_____

Recipe:

Preparation Time: _____ Serves: _____

Oven Temp: _____ Cooking Time: _____

Ingredients

_____ _____

_____ _____

_____ _____

_____ _____

_____ _____

_____ _____

_____ _____

_____ _____

Method

_____

_____

_____

_____

_____

_____

_____

_____

Notes

_____

_____

_____

_____

_____

Recipe: _____

Preparation Time: _____   Serves: ____

Oven Temp: _____ Cooking Time: ____

Ingredients

_____   _____

_____   _____

_____   _____

_____   _____

_____   _____

_____   _____

_____   _____

Method

_____

_____

_____

_____

_____

_____

_____

_____

Notes

_____

_____

_____

_____

_____

Recipe: _____

Preparation Time: _____   Serves: _____

Oven Temp: _____ Cooking Time: _____

Ingredients

_____ _____
_____ _____
_____ _____
_____ _____
_____ _____
_____ _____
_____ _____

Method

_____
_____
_____
_____
_____
_____
_____
_____

Notes

_____
_____
_____
_____
_____

Recipe: _____

Preparation Time: _____ Serves: _____

Oven Temp: _____ Cooking Time: _____

Ingredients

_____   _____
_____   _____
_____   _____
_____   _____
_____   _____
_____   _____
_____   _____
_____   _____

Method

_____
_____
_____
_____
_____
_____
_____
_____
_____

Notes

_____
_____
_____
_____
_____

Recipe: _____

Preparation Time: _____   Serves: _____

Oven Temp: _____ Cooking Time: _____

Ingredients

_____   _____
_____   _____
_____   _____
_____   _____
_____   _____
_____   _____
_____   _____

Method

_____
_____
_____
_____
_____
_____
_____
_____

Notes

_____
_____
_____
_____
_____

Recipe: _____

Preparation Time: _____   Serves: _____

Oven Temp: _____ Cooking Time: _____

Ingredients

_____   _____

_____   _____

_____   _____

_____   _____

_____   _____

_____   _____

_____   _____

Method

_____

_____

_____

_____

_____

_____

_____

_____

_____

Notes

_____

_____

_____

_____

_____

Recipe: _____

Preparation Time: _____ Serves: _____

Oven Temp: _____ Cooking Time: _____

Ingredients

_____ _____

_____ _____

_____ _____

_____ _____

_____ _____

_____ _____

_____ _____

_____

Method

_____

_____

_____

_____

_____

_____

_____

_____

_____

Notes

_____

_____

_____

_____

_____

Recipe: _____

Preparation Time: _____ Serves: _____

Oven Temp: _____ Cooking Time: _____

Ingredients

_____ _____
_____ _____
_____ _____
_____ _____
_____ _____
_____ _____
_____ _____

Method

_____
_____
_____
_____
_____
_____
_____
_____

Notes

_____
_____
_____
_____
_____

Recipe: _____

Preparation Time: _____   Serves: _____

Oven Temp: _____ Cooking Time: _____

Ingredients

_____   _____

_____   _____

_____   _____

_____   _____

_____   _____

_____   _____

_____   _____

Method

_____

_____

_____

_____

_____

_____

_____

_____

Notes

_____

_____

_____

_____

_____

Recipe:

Preparation Time:_____   Serves:_____

Oven Temp:_____ Cooking Time:_____

Ingredients

_____   _____
_____   _____
_____   _____
_____   _____
_____   _____
_____   _____
_____   _____

Method

_____
_____
_____
_____
_____
_____
_____
_____
_____

Notes

_____
_____
_____
_____
_____

Recipe:

Preparation Time: _____ Serves: _____

Oven Temp: _____ Cooking Time: _____

Ingredients

_____ _____

_____ _____

_____ _____

_____ _____

_____ _____

_____ _____

_____

Method

_____

_____

_____

_____

_____

_____

_____

_____

Notes

_____

_____

_____

_____

_____

Recipe:

Preparation Time: _____ Serves: _____

Oven Temp: _____ Cooking Time: _____

Ingredients

_____   _____
_____   _____
_____   _____
_____   _____
_____   _____
_____   _____
_____   _____

Method

_____
_____
_____
_____
_____
_____
_____
_____

Notes

_____
_____
_____
_____
_____

Recipe: _____

Preparation Time: _____ Serves: _____

Oven Temp: _____ Cooking Time: _____

Ingredients

_____ _____

_____ _____

_____ _____

_____ _____

_____ _____

_____ _____

_____ _____

Method

_____

_____

_____

_____

_____

_____

_____

_____

Notes

_____

_____

_____

_____

_____

Recipe: _____

Preparation Time: _____ Serves: _____

Oven Temp: _____ Cooking Time: _____

Ingredients

_____ _____

_____ _____

_____ _____

_____ _____

_____ _____

_____ _____

_____ _____

Method

_____

_____

_____

_____

_____

_____

_____

_____

Notes

_____

_____

_____

_____

_____

Recipe: _____

Preparation Time: _____ Serves: _____

Oven Temp: _____ Cooking Time: _____

Ingredients

_____ _____
_____ _____
_____ _____
_____ _____
_____ _____
_____ _____
_____ _____
_____

Method

_____
_____
_____
_____
_____
_____
_____
_____
_____

Notes

_____
_____
_____
_____
_____

Recipe: _____

Preparation Time: _____   Serves: _____

Oven Temp: _____ Cooking Time: _____

Ingredients

_____   _____

_____   _____

_____   _____

_____   _____

_____   _____

_____   _____

_____   _____

Method

_____

_____

_____

_____

_____

_____

_____

_____

_____

Notes

_____

_____

_____

_____

_____

Recipe:

Preparation Time: _____   Serves: _____

Oven Temp: _____ Cooking Time: _____

Ingredients

_____   _____
_____   _____
_____   _____
_____   _____
_____   _____
_____   _____
_____   _____

Method

_____
_____
_____
_____
_____
_____
_____
_____

Notes

_____
_____
_____
_____
_____

Recipe:

Preparation Time: _____   Serves: _____

Oven Temp: _____ Cooking Time: _____

Ingredients

_____   _____
_____   _____
_____   _____
_____   _____
_____   _____
_____   _____
_____   _____

Method

_____
_____
_____
_____
_____
_____
_____
_____
_____

Notes

_____
_____
_____
_____
_____

Recipe:

Preparation Time: _____ Serves: _____

Oven Temp: _____ Cooking Time: _____

Ingredients

_____   _____

_____   _____

_____   _____

_____   _____

_____   _____

_____   _____

_____   _____

Method

Notes

Recipe: _____

Preparation Time: _____   Serves: _____

Oven Temp: _____ Cooking Time: _____

Ingredients

_____   _____
_____   _____
_____   _____
_____   _____
_____   _____
_____   _____
_____   _____

Method

_____
_____
_____
_____
_____
_____
_____
_____
_____

Notes

_____
_____
_____
_____
_____

Recipe: _____

Preparation Time: _____   Serves: _____

Oven Temp: _____ Cooking Time: _____

Ingredients

_____   _____
_____   _____
_____   _____
_____   _____
_____   _____
_____   _____
_____   _____
_____

Method

_____
_____
_____
_____
_____
_____
_____
_____
_____

Notes

_____
_____
_____
_____
_____

Recipe: _____

Preparation Time: _____   Serves: _____

Oven Temp: _____ Cooking Time: _____

Ingredients

_____   _____
_____   _____
_____   _____
_____   _____
_____   _____
_____   _____
_____   _____

Method

_____
_____
_____
_____
_____
_____
_____
_____
_____

Notes

_____
_____
_____
_____
_____

Recipe: _____

Preparation Time: _____ Serves: _____

Oven Temp: _____ Cooking Time: _____

Ingredients

_____ _____
_____ _____
_____ _____
_____ _____
_____ _____
_____ _____
_____ _____
_____

Method

_____
_____
_____
_____
_____
_____
_____
_____

Notes

_____
_____
_____
_____
_____

Recipe: _____

Preparation Time: _____ Serves: _____

Oven Temp: _____ Cooking Time: _____

Ingredients

_____ _____
_____ _____
_____ _____
_____ _____
_____ _____
_____ _____
_____ _____

Method

_____
_____
_____
_____
_____
_____
_____
_____

Notes

_____
_____
_____
_____
_____

Recipe: _____

Preparation Time: _____   Serves: _____

Oven Temp: _____ Cooking Time: _____

Ingredients

_____   _____

_____   _____

_____   _____

_____   _____

_____   _____

_____   _____

_____   _____

_____   _____

Method

_____

_____

_____

_____

_____

_____

_____

_____

_____

Notes

_____

_____

_____

_____

_____

Recipe: _____

Preparation Time: _____   Serves: _____

Oven Temp: _____ Cooking Time: _____

Ingredients

_____   _____
_____   _____
_____   _____
_____   _____
_____   _____
_____   _____
_____   _____
_____   _____

Method

_____
_____
_____
_____
_____
_____
_____
_____
_____

Notes

_____
_____
_____
_____
_____

Recipe: _____

Preparation Time: _____ Serves: _____

Oven Temp: _____ Cooking Time: _____

Ingredients

_____ _____

_____ _____

_____ _____

_____ _____

_____ _____

_____ _____

_____

Method

_____

_____

_____

_____

_____

_____

_____

_____

_____

Notes

_____

_____

_____

_____

_____

Recipe: _____

Preparation Time: _____   Serves: _____

Oven Temp: _____ Cooking Time: _____

Ingredients

_____   _____
_____   _____
_____   _____
_____   _____
_____   _____
_____   _____
_____   _____

Method

_____
_____
_____
_____
_____
_____
_____
_____

Notes

_____
_____
_____
_____
_____

Recipe: _____

Preparation Time: _____   Serves: _____

Oven Temp: _____ Cooking Time: _____

Ingredients

_____   _____

_____   _____

_____   _____

_____   _____

_____   _____

_____   _____

_____   _____

Method

_____

_____

_____

_____

_____

_____

_____

_____

Notes

_____

_____

_____

_____

_____

Recipe:

Preparation Time: _____ Serves: ____

Oven Temp: _____ Cooking Time: ____

Ingredients

_____ _____
_____ _____
_____ _____
_____ _____
_____ _____
_____ _____
_____ _____
_____ _____

Method

Notes

Recipe: _____

Preparation Time: _____   Serves: _____

Oven Temp: _____ Cooking Time: _____

Ingredients

_____   _____
_____   _____
_____   _____
_____   _____
_____   _____
_____   _____
_____   _____
_____   _____

Method

_____
_____
_____
_____
_____
_____
_____
_____

Notes

_____
_____
_____
_____
_____

Recipe: _____

Preparation Time: _____ Serves: _____

Oven Temp: _____ Cooking Time: _____

Ingredients

_____ _____

_____ _____

_____ _____

_____ _____

_____ _____

_____ _____

_____ _____

Method

_____

_____

_____

_____

_____

_____

_____

_____

_____

Notes

_____

_____

_____

_____

_____

Recipe: _____

Preparation Time: _____ Serves: _____

Oven Temp: _____ Cooking Time: _____

Ingredients

_____   _____
_____   _____
_____   _____
_____   _____
_____   _____
_____   _____
_____   _____
_____

Method

_____
_____
_____
_____
_____
_____
_____
_____
_____

Notes

_____
_____
_____
_____
_____

Recipe: _____

Preparation Time: _____ Serves: _____

Oven Temp: _____ Cooking Time: _____

Ingredients

_____ _____
_____ _____
_____ _____
_____ _____
_____ _____
_____ _____
_____

Method

_____
_____
_____
_____
_____
_____
_____
_____
_____

Notes

_____
_____
_____
_____
_____

Recipe:

Preparation Time:_____   Serves:____

Oven Temp:_____ Cooking Time:____

Ingredients

_____   _____
_____   _____
_____   _____
_____   _____
_____   _____
_____   _____
_____   _____

Method

_____
_____
_____
_____
_____
_____
_____
_____
_____

Notes

_____
_____
_____
_____
_____

Recipe:

Preparation Time:_____   Serves:_____

Oven Temp:_____ Cooking Time:_____

Ingredients

_____   _____
_____   _____
_____   _____
_____   _____
_____   _____
_____   _____
_____   _____

Method

_____
_____
_____
_____
_____
_____
_____
_____
_____

Notes

_____
_____
_____
_____
_____

47

Recipe:

Preparation Time: _____   Serves: _____

Oven Temp: _____ Cooking Time: _____

Ingredients

_____   _____

_____   _____

_____   _____

_____   _____

_____   _____

_____   _____

_____   _____

Method

Notes

Recipe:

Preparation Time: _____   Serves: _____

Oven Temp: _____ Cooking Time: _____

Ingredients

_____   _____
_____   _____
_____   _____
_____   _____
_____   _____
_____   _____
_____   _____

Method

_____
_____
_____
_____
_____
_____
_____
_____
_____

Notes

_____
_____
_____
_____
_____

Recipe:

Preparation Time:_____ Serves:_____

Oven Temp:_____ Cooking Time:_____

Ingredients

Method

Notes

Recipe: _____

Preparation Time: _____   Serves: _____

Oven Temp: _____ Cooking Time: _____

Ingredients

_____   _____
_____   _____
_____   _____
_____   _____
_____   _____
_____   _____
_____

Method

_____
_____
_____
_____
_____
_____
_____
_____
_____

Notes

_____
_____
_____
_____
_____

Recipe: _____

Preparation Time: _____   Serves: _____

Oven Temp: _____ Cooking Time: _____

Ingredients

_____ _____
_____ _____
_____ _____
_____ _____
_____ _____
_____ _____
_____ _____
_____

Method

_____
_____
_____
_____
_____
_____
_____
_____
_____

Notes

_____
_____
_____
_____
_____

Recipe:

Preparation Time: _____ Serves: _____

Oven Temp: _____ Cooking Time: _____

Ingredients

_____   _____
_____   _____
_____   _____
_____   _____
_____   _____
_____   _____
_____   _____
_____

Method

Notes

Recipe: _____

Preparation Time: _____   Serves: _____

Oven Temp: _____ Cooking Time: _____

Ingredients

_____   _____
_____   _____
_____   _____
_____   _____
_____   _____
_____   _____
_____   _____
_____   _____

Method

_____
_____
_____
_____
_____
_____
_____
_____
_____

Notes

_____
_____
_____
_____
_____

Recipe:

Preparation Time:_____   Serves:_____

Oven Temp:_____ Cooking Time:_____

Ingredients

_____   _____
_____   _____
_____   _____
_____   _____
_____   _____
_____   _____
_____   _____

Method

_____
_____
_____
_____
_____
_____
_____
_____
_____

Notes

_____
_____
_____
_____
_____

Recipe: _____

Preparation Time: _____ Serves: _____

Oven Temp: _____ Cooking Time: _____

Ingredients

_____ _____
_____ _____
_____ _____
_____ _____
_____ _____
_____ _____
_____ _____
_____

Method

_____
_____
_____
_____
_____
_____
_____
_____
_____

Notes

_____
_____
_____
_____
_____

Recipe:

Preparation Time:_____ Serves:_____

Oven Temp:_____ Cooking Time:_____

Ingredients

_____ _____
_____ _____
_____ _____
_____ _____
_____ _____
_____ _____
_____

Method

_____
_____
_____
_____
_____
_____
_____
_____
_____

Notes

_____
_____
_____
_____
_____

Recipe: _____

Preparation Time: _____ Serves: _____

Oven Temp: _____ Cooking Time: _____

Ingredients

_____ _____
_____ _____
_____ _____
_____ _____
_____ _____
_____ _____
_____ _____

Method

_____
_____
_____
_____
_____
_____
_____
_____

Notes

_____
_____
_____
_____
_____

Recipe:

Preparation Time: _____ Serves: _____

Oven Temp: _____ Cooking Time: _____

Ingredients

_____ _____

_____ _____

_____ _____

_____ _____

_____ _____

_____ _____

_____ _____

Method

_____

_____

_____

_____

_____

_____

_____

_____

Notes

_____

_____

_____

_____

_____

Recipe: _____

Preparation Time: _____   Serves: _____

Oven Temp: _____ Cooking Time: _____

Ingredients

_____   _____
_____   _____
_____   _____
_____   _____
_____   _____
_____   _____
_____   _____
_____

Method

_____
_____
_____
_____
_____
_____
_____
_____

Notes

_____
_____
_____
_____
_____

Recipe: _____

Preparation Time: _____   Serves: _____

Oven Temp: _____ Cooking Time: _____

Ingredients

_____   _____
_____   _____
_____   _____
_____   _____
_____   _____
_____   _____
_____   _____

Method

_____
_____
_____
_____
_____
_____
_____
_____
_____

Notes

_____
_____
_____
_____
_____

Recipe:

Preparation Time: _____ Serves: _____

Oven Temp: _____ Cooking Time: _____

Ingredients

_____ _____
_____ _____
_____ _____
_____ _____
_____ _____
_____ _____
_____ _____

Method

_____
_____
_____
_____
_____
_____
_____
_____
_____

Notes

_____
_____
_____
_____
_____

Recipe: _____

Preparation Time: _____ Serves: _____

Oven Temp: _____ Cooking Time: _____

Ingredients

_____ _____

_____ _____

_____ _____

_____ _____

_____ _____

_____ _____

_____ _____

Method

_____

_____

_____

_____

_____

_____

_____

_____

Notes

_____

_____

_____

_____

_____

Recipe: _____

Preparation Time: _____   Serves: _____

Oven Temp: _____ Cooking Time: _____

Ingredients

_____   _____
_____   _____
_____   _____
_____   _____
_____   _____
_____   _____
_____   _____
_____   _____

Method

_____
_____
_____
_____
_____
_____
_____
_____

Notes

_____
_____
_____
_____
_____

Recipe: _____

Preparation Time: _____   Serves: _____

Oven Temp: _____ Cooking Time: _____

Ingredients

_____   _____
_____   _____
_____   _____
_____   _____
_____   _____
_____   _____
_____   _____

Method

Notes

65

Recipe: _____

Preparation Time: _____ Serves: _____

Oven Temp: _____ Cooking Time: _____

Ingredients

_____ _____
_____ _____
_____ _____
_____ _____
_____ _____
_____ _____
_____ _____

Method

_____
_____
_____
_____
_____
_____
_____
_____

Notes

_____
_____
_____
_____
_____

Recipe: _____

Preparation Time: _____   Serves: _____

Oven Temp: _____ Cooking Time: _____

Ingredients

_____   _____
_____   _____
_____   _____
_____   _____
_____   _____
_____   _____
_____   _____
_____

Method

_____
_____
_____
_____
_____
_____
_____
_____
_____
_____

Notes

_____
_____
_____
_____
_____

Recipe:

Preparation Time: _____ Serves: _____

Oven Temp: _____ Cooking Time: _____

Ingredients

_____ _____

_____ _____

_____ _____

_____ _____

_____ _____

_____ _____

_____ _____

Method

_____

_____

_____

_____

_____

_____

_____

_____

Notes

_____

_____

_____

_____

_____

Recipe: _____

Preparation Time: _____   Serves: ____

Oven Temp: _____ Cooking Time: ____

Ingredients

_____   _____
_____   _____
_____   _____
_____   _____
_____   _____
_____   _____
_____   _____

Method

_____
_____
_____
_____
_____
_____
_____
_____
_____

Notes

_____
_____
_____
_____
_____

Recipe: _____

Preparation Time: _____ Serves: _____

Oven Temp: _____ Cooking Time: _____

Ingredients

_____   _____
_____   _____
_____   _____
_____   _____
_____   _____
_____   _____
_____   _____

Method

_____
_____
_____
_____
_____
_____
_____
_____
_____

Notes

_____
_____
_____
_____
_____

Recipe:

Preparation Time: _____ Serves: _____

Oven Temp: _____ Cooking Time: _____

Ingredients

_____ _____
_____ _____
_____ _____
_____ _____
_____ _____
_____ _____
_____ _____

Method

_____
_____
_____
_____
_____
_____
_____
_____
_____

Notes

_____
_____
_____
_____
_____

Recipe: _____

Preparation Time: _____   Serves: _____

Oven Temp: _____ Cooking Time: _____

Ingredients

_____   _____
_____   _____
_____   _____
_____   _____
_____   _____
_____   _____
_____   _____
_____

Method

_____
_____
_____
_____
_____
_____
_____
_____
_____

Notes

_____
_____
_____
_____
_____

Recipe:

Preparation Time: _____ Serves: _____

Oven Temp: _____ Cooking Time: _____

Ingredients

Method

Notes

Recipe:

Preparation Time: _____   Serves: _____

Oven Temp: _____ Cooking Time: _____

Ingredients

_____   _____
_____   _____
_____   _____
_____   _____
_____   _____
_____   _____
_____   _____

Method

Notes

Recipe:

Preparation Time: _____ Serves: _____

Oven Temp: _____ Cooking Time: _____

Ingredients

_____ _____
_____ _____
_____ _____
_____ _____
_____ _____
_____ _____
_____ _____

Method

_____
_____
_____
_____
_____
_____
_____
_____
_____

Notes

_____
_____
_____
_____
_____

Recipe: _____

Preparation Time: _____   Serves: _____

Oven Temp: _____ Cooking Time: _____

Ingredients

_____ _____
_____ _____
_____ _____
_____ _____
_____ _____
_____ _____
_____ _____

Method

_____
_____
_____
_____
_____
_____
_____
_____
_____

Notes

_____
_____
_____
_____
_____

Recipe: _____

Preparation Time: _____   Serves: _____

Oven Temp: _____ Cooking Time: _____

Ingredients

_____   _____
_____   _____
_____   _____
_____   _____
_____   _____
_____   _____
_____   _____

Method

_____
_____
_____
_____
_____
_____
_____
_____
_____

Notes

_____
_____
_____
_____
_____

Recipe: _____

Preparation Time: _____   Serves: _____

Oven Temp: _____ Cooking Time: _____

Ingredients

_____   _____

_____   _____

_____   _____

_____   _____

_____   _____

_____   _____

_____

Method

_____

_____

_____

_____

_____

_____

_____

_____

Notes

_____

_____

_____

_____

_____

Recipe: _____

Preparation Time: _____ Serves: _____

Oven Temp: _____ Cooking Time: _____

Ingredients

_____	_____
_____	_____
_____	_____
_____	_____
_____	_____
_____	_____
_____	_____

Method

_____

_____

_____

_____

_____

_____

_____

_____

Notes

_____

_____

_____

_____

_____

Recipe: _____

Preparation Time: _____ Serves: _____

Oven Temp: _____ Cooking Time: _____

Ingredients

_____ _____

_____ _____

_____ _____

_____ _____

_____ _____

_____ _____

_____

Method

_____

_____

_____

_____

_____

_____

_____

_____

Notes

_____

_____

_____

_____

Printed in Great Britain
by Amazon

263b13a3-d020-42a0-92ae-088ea86cb123R01